Luminous Mountain

WRITTEN BY

MARCELA GRANT

To Janah,

With Love, Beauty and Light.

Marcela

ILLUSTRATED BY PATRICIA MOFFETT

LUMINOUS MOUNTAIN
MARCELA GRANT

Copyright © 2011 Marcela Grant

ILLUSTRATIONS
Patricia Moffett

EDITOR AND PUBLICITY
Elizabeth McBlain

ART DIRECTION
Marcela Grant

DESIGN AND LAYOUT
Marcela Grant

Balboa Press books may be ordered through booksellers or by contacting:

Balboa Press
A Division of Hay House
1663 Liberty Drive
Bloomington, IN 47403
www.balboapress.com
1-(877) 407-4847

ISBN: 978-1-4525-3466-4 (sc)

Library of Congress Control Number: 2011906710

Printed in the United States of America

Balboa Press rev. date: 5/6/2011

Words of Praise

"A gorgeous and inspiring book, uplifting, enchanting, and transforming. As the journey unfolds you feel like springtime is awakening within you. I highly recommend it."

Alberto Villoldo *PhD*
Bestselling author of Shaman, Healer, Sage.

"This powerful story of a child's journey not only takes us on our own journey of discovering inner strength and growth, but it brings forth ancient wisdoms that have guided us for thousands of years, of a way to live with peace and harmony within ourselves and our world."

Heidi McBratney
Medicine Woman

To my Family

To my son, *Seth*, I dedicate this story to you. You are the inspiration for the main character 'Justin.' May this book remind you that *your life* is a wonderful journey. Walk your path with strength and compassion. Recognize and honor the light that shines within you. This light, I see in your beautiful eyes.

You are never alone, I am always with you.

Love, Mommy

To my daughter, *Hope*, for you I am writing a sequel, *Luminous Rose*. May you walk with beauty around you and *your inner light* shine brightly, always. Your inner beauty is a precious gift from above. Protect and nourish the sweetness that lives in your heart.

You are the sweetness in my life, forever and always.

Love, Mommy

To my husband, *Mark*, I am grateful and feel blessed for all the love and support you have given me throughout our journey together. Allow *your soul* to be free, spread your wings and fly.

It is your soul my heart belongs to.

Love, Marcela

CHAPTER ONE

The sun was shining on his soft and gentle face, his large beautiful brown eyes sparkled in the sunlight, and his dark brown hair blew in the soft breeze. The day was warm and the air was filled with the scent from the sweet flowers nearby. Justin was a happy nine year old. He laid flat on his back in the tall green grass of the meadow and watched the clouds drift by. He giggled as he looked at the clouds and imagined what kind of animals they looked like to him. Justin enjoyed these special times alone with his mother, since his mother's attention was usually shared with his twin sister, Julia. He looked to his side where his mother laid beside him smiling back at him. There was no other place where he would rather be.

The warmth of the sun touched his delicate skin as he gently fell asleep.

A cold breeze swept by and gave him chills. As he opened his eyes, he saw the sky had grown into dark clouds. He reached for his mother, but she was not there. Rain harshly fell on his little body. Rumbling thunder shook the clouds, vibrating in his ears, and lightening electrified the sky. He called out to his mother but his voice faded in the sounds of the storm. The beauty of the sunny meadow was gone.

He panicked and looked in different directions looking for his mother. He knew he needed to find shelter; perhaps his mother would be there, waiting with open arms to comfort and protect him. Not knowing where he was going, he ran, and ran ...

His heart pounded faster and faster. Justin wondered, "Where's my mom? ... How could she leave me?"... Tears ran down his face.

Justin came upon a mountain and noticed an opening. It was dark and he was scared, there was no way he was going inside the cave. Lightening struck a cherry blossom tree close by. Startled, Justin ran and jumped into the cave. He was frightened by the echoing sounds inside the cave. He felt as though the cave knew him somehow and was trying to communicate with him. With great disappointment he realized that his mother was not in the cave.

CHAPTER TWO

Justin became angry at himself for getting lost. He was confused and could not understand how his mother could abandon him. Justin was sad and angry, feeling very alone.

The silence seemed to speak to him; he thought he heard a sound... "Hiss."

Justin froze as he recognized the sound. He slowly turned his head to see where the sound was coming from. Far in a dark corner, a serpent poked her head out into the light. Justin was surprised to see how beautiful this serpent looked. She had silky black skin; she slithered gracefully and softly on the earth. Her eyes were gentle, and Justin was not afraid of her.

"Hello, my name is Sasha."

Justin was surprised to hear the serpent speak.

"You seem to be lost," said Sasha.

"I can't find my mom. Have you seen her?" Justin asked.

"Yes, I have," the serpent replied, "she was on her way to *Luminous Mountain*."

"*Luminous Mountain*, what is that?" Justin wondered.

"The spirit of the sacred mountains is the most powerful of all nature spirits. *Luminous Mountain* is a sacred mountain that almost reaches the heavens; it is the place to attain enlightenment. The journey to *Luminous Mountain* is a courageous one."

"What is enlightenment?" Justin questioned.

"Enlightenment is finding the *Light* within you. It means, to let your soul fly free with peace and beauty. Love and embrace all of God's creations, all of Mother Nature's beauty; the stones, the plants, the animals, the birds and the tiny creatures; all living together in harmony and peace. To obtain the understanding that we are all one, called the Universe."

"How do I get there? I don't know the way!" Justin cried anxiously.

"I can help you part of the way. My friends await to take you the rest of your journey," Sasha assured him.

"What friends?" Justin asked with curiosity.

"My sacred friends, power animals. You will meet them when you are ready," Sasha added.

"What are power animals?" Justin questioned.

"These are animals that bring power and wisdom. They are spirits that empower and protect, similar to guardian angels," Sasha answered.

Justin sat down on the ground, the cave was cold, but at least it was dry. He felt sleepy but he was too scared to surrender to his exhaustion. He shivered. Sasha slithered slowly towards him trying not to frighten him.

"You seem cold, I can help keep you warm," Sasha offered.

Justin was not sure how he felt about having a serpent keeping him warm, but she seemed harmless. He hesitated for a few minutes and then accepted Sasha's offer. Sasha gently wrapped her coils around him. The warmth and softness of her silky skin felt as though his mother was putting her arms around him embracing and keeping him safe. He wondered if his mother was missing him as much as he missed her.

With one great sigh, he breathed deeply and fell asleep.

CHAPTER THREE

The next morning, the sun shone through the tiny openings of the cave, the sky was clear and blue. The rain had enhanced the sweet fragrance of the flowers in the summer breeze. The clouds and sky were beautiful and peaceful again. He looked for Sasha, and saw her outside in the meadow, near a couple of big rocks.

"Good morning friend, I hope you slept well," said Sasha.

Justin was still trying to get over the fact that he was actually talking with a snake. "Hmm, I guess so."

Sasha looked at him with kind eyes, "You still seem sad."

Justin felt very sad, but also he was angry at himself and his mother. "It is my fault for getting lost," he paced back and forth, "but she left me!" Sasha moved closer and Justin whispered to her, "I wish she was still with me." Sasha replied, "She is still with you, in your heart."

Sasha paused for a moment to give Justin time to honor his feelings. She then continued, "Today is the day! The day when I shed my skin and let go of all my damaged skin that I no longer need. Today I renew myself... Today can be your day to renew yourself too."

Justin was not clear what she had meant. He could not shed his skin, that would be painful! He knew that talking to a serpent was silly, but now it was becoming crazy. "I can't do that!" he protested.

"I am a serpent and you are a boy, we are both different and yet we come from the same place. We are all part of the Oneness. I shed my skin to renew myself, you can shed your past experiences and hurtful feelings to renew yourself in a different way." Justin thought for a while... and then asked, "How?"

Sasha slithered towards the two rocks nearby; she squeezed in between them and seemed to disappear. All Justin could see was the serpent's thin layer of skin that was left behind. He worried Sasha was hurt. As he jumped to look for her, he saw Sasha coming around the other side of the rocks. Her skin was no longer silky, like he had remembered, but even more beautiful than he could have imagined. The sun shone on her black skin and illuminated it.

She looked like a shimmering jewel. She moved towards him a little faster this time and with excitement. "I feel great! Your turn now."

Justin exclaimed, "I can't fit between those rocks."

Sasha giggled, "Of course not silly, you are not a serpent."

Sasha continued, "Try this, close your eyes and remember how you felt when you got lost and could not find your mother, the feelings of fear, anger and sadness. Now take a deep breath and blow the energy of these feelings into the rocks. Next, lie down on the ground, belly to belly with Pachamama."

"Who is Pachamama?" Justin asked.

"Pachamama is Mother Earth; the Goddess responsible for the well-being of plants and animals. She has the power to mulch and renew. Everything that returns to her soil becomes one with all life forms; the birds, the trees, the stones; creating new life. Ask Pachamama to take these feelings of fear, anger and sadness away from you. She will absorb them into her rich soil and transform them into beautiful flowers."

Justin followed Sasha's directions. He was surprised how easy it was to release these emotions into the rocks. When he lay down on the earth, Justin felt Pachamama embracing him with love and protection. He could feel Mother Earth's heart beat. He looked around and noticed white daisies surrounding him. Daisies were his mother's favorite flowers. Perhaps, this was a sign from Pachamama that his mother was still with him. He felt so much lighter, happier and calmer now.

"Well, I must be going now," Sasha said.

"But, wait! Justin sounded alarm, "you can't leave me now. How am I going to get to *Luminous Mountain*?"

Sasha spoke in a calm tone, "Now that you have renewed yourself, you are now ready for the rest of your journey. Don't worry, you will have company." Sasha swirled softly around Justin. "It was my pleasure to be a part of your journey." Then she slipped away.

Justin called out to her. "Goodbye Sasha ... By the way my name is Justin."

Sasha replied, "I know."

CHAPTER FOUR

Justin started to walk, hoping to find the path to *Luminous Mountain*. He longed for his mother's embrace. He didn't know what he needed to do next. Sasha said that her power animal friends will help him, but he couldn't see anyone. The meadow seemed uninhabited. One thing he was certain of was that he was hungry!

The meadow came to an end. There was only a forest in front of him. Justin entered the forest realizing it was actually a jungle, a magical world. This was a world full of light and wondrous life. Exotic hanging gardens overhead, brilliantly colored flowers and trees covered with ripe fruits. However, this spectacular kingdom was also dark, damp and full of dangerous and unknown wildlife.

Justin wanted to eat the fruits but was scared they may be poisonous. He couldn't sit down without being bitten by the armies of ants. Even more frightening, were the strange sounds of the jungle and its creatures. Nothing was as it appeared.

Justin walked aimlessly for a while. He followed what seemed to be a trail of some kind. The trail led him to a hidden den. Outside the entrance of the den, he saw a gathering of food. He approached towards it excited and cautiously. In a flash, a white wolf leapt out of the den, protecting its territory. Startled, Justin lost his footing and balance and fell on his back. Justin got up and started to run away from the wolf quickly. The white wolf chased him to the edge of the river. The river was wide and too deep to walk through it. A fallen old tree trunk lay across the river. Justin carefully jumped onto the tree trunk and started to cross over. He looked back cautiously to see if the wolf was following him. The white wolf stopped at the edge of the river. Justin felt relieved and then suddenly he lost his balance and began struggling to keep a grip on the old tree. The wolf, in a careful but determined way, started to approach him again. At that moment, a magnificent spotted creature leapt out in the air, gracefully and quickly. It jumped across the river, chasing and scaring the wolf away. Justin regained his balance and managed to finish crossing the unstable bridge and reached the other side exhausted and relieved.

The Jaguar was powerful and beautiful, tanned with distinctive black spots shaped like roses. The large cat slowly made his way to Justin.

"Hello Justin, Sasha told me that you were coming. My name is Otorongo; I am the caretaker of the jungle."

Justin was happy to meet one of Sasha's friends, especially one who could protect him so fearlessly. "I am glad you came to help me, I was so afraid. Will you stay to guide and protect me?"

Otorongo replied, "I will stay with you until you have learned the lessons you need for your journey."

Before Justin could reply, he became aware that he had lost the blue crystal his mother had given him. It must have fallen out when he fell by the den when the white wolf jumped towards him. He started to cry, this crystal was very special to him. His mother had given it to him to help him feel calm and loved. This was all he had left of her. "Oh no! I must find my crystal, I must go back!" Otorongo could see Justin was deeply upset. "Everything will work out, my little man. I will help you track and find it. First you need to gain your strength." Justin's head hung down in sadness as tears fell upon his cheeks. Otorongo moved closer and gently licked Justin's tears from his face.

Moving slowly through the dense jungle, Otorongo taught Justin the secrets of his environment. Justin learned to choose safe, healthy foods and clean drinking water. He taught him important lessons like how to prevent from insect bites, avoiding heatstroke and dehydration. He even showed him how to avoid being tracked by dangerous animals.

Otorongo told Justin, "When you are connected to all livings things and respect Mother Earth, you become in balance with the flow of the Universe. When you enter the jungle with pure intentions, the jungle will accept you, and provide for you.

CHAPTER FIVE

That night after Justin had finished eating until he was satisfied, Otorongo found a large tree with strong, sturdy branches to climb. At first, Justin was fearful of the tree's height and uncertain of his ability to climb such a large tree. They climbed as high as they could go so they could sleep safely through the night. Justin gazed at the brilliant stars in the sky. He looked down below and saw how much smaller the jungle had become beneath him. The sounds of the wildlife seemed to lessen in the darkness of the night, all was calm and quiet.

In a small voice, Justin asked Otorongo, "You are very strong and fierce; you could have easily hurt the wolf. Why didn't you?"

Otorongo replied, "I do not engage in violence or attack because I can. The wolf was only protecting its territory. To be truly powerful, one needs to practice integrity and peace. I am a Luminous Warrior; one who is strong, courageous and has no enemies in this world or the next. I walk the path across the Rainbow Bridge."

"What is the Rainbow Bridge?" Justin asked.

"The Rainbow Bridge is the path to the world of mystery and peace. I can take you there if you would like. When you hold on to feelings of anger, fear and grief, you prevent moving forward on your journey. First, you need to transform these heavy emotions into energies of light and sources of strength." Otorongo said encouragingly.

Justin asked, "How do I do that?"

"By stepping beyond fear and violence; when you no longer respond from a place of anger, then you are practicing peace for yourself and others. Trust your spirit," Otorongo said.

Justin thought for a while about Otorongo's teachings. Justin began to understand these lessons into his way of being. He felt that he was beginning to become one with the Universe. He looked up into the starry sky and fell asleep.

Early in the morning, Otorongo lead the way back to the den, to find Justin's blue crystal. Justin was concerned that

Otorongo had taken a different path. "This is not the right way!" Justin called out.

Otorongo replied, "There are many paths you can take to arrive at one destination."

Along the journey they came upon the river and saw a radiant Rainbow Bridge connected to the other side. The bridge looked like a luminous arc with red, orange, yellow, green, blue, indigo and violet hues spread across the sky as the sun shone on it brightly. As they walked over the bridge, Justin felt renewed in this light.

Otorongo and Justin peacefully approached the den. As they reached the den they saw the white wolf nursing her cubs. She sensed Otorongo posed no harm, she also felt Justin had transformed and had become one with nature. Justin sat on the ground and was mesmerized by the cute little cubs, and now could appreciate the beautiful mother wolf. He understood all of Otorongo's lessons.

While Justin sat, some of the wolf cubs came to him excitedly, wanting to play. Justin smiled and found delight in the moment, enjoying the innocence and purity of it all.

As Justin and Otorongo started to leave, the mother wolf

came to Justin. This time he was not afraid of her. He kneeled down to gently pet her but she seemed to want to lick his palm. He let her, and watched in amazement as she gently opened her mouth and placed his special blue crystal on his palm. Justin rejoiced...

Otorongo whispered to him, "Justin you have gained much wisdom. You are ready to continue your journey and create your own path. It has been my honor to show you the ways of the Luminous Warrior. From this point on, you carry me within you." Justin felt his eyes filling up with tears; he had grown very fond of Otorongo. He remembered Sasha telling him that he would meet other friends on his journey, but he was still sad to say goodbye. Otorongo taught him well, he had to trust that *his spirit* will lead the way. Justin put his arms around Otorongo and held him closely. Justin hoped that Otorongo knew how much he meant to him. Otorongo licked Justin's face and with one leap into the air he disappeared back into the jungle.

CHAPTER SIX

Justin continued on his journey to *Luminous Mountain*. He felt courageous and powerful, now that he walked the path of the Luminous Warrior.

Justin walked, proceeding with a purpose. He entered a path in the forest, this time it was different from the first time he walked in the jungle alone, he was not scared. He noticed the trees hanging overhead; he felt the moist soft ground beneath his feet. He was aware of all the sounds and the smells of the jungle. As he moved along, Justin saw a clearing ahead. He made his way through the path and left the jungle behind. Upon entering this new place, he became aware that an enchanted garden awaited.

He ventured into the fairy-tale garden with tall majestic trees. A multitude of beautiful flowers stretched across this magical garden as far as he could see. Rose petals and butterflies danced together on the wind. Justin heard the sound of water; he turned his head toward the sound and discovered a waterfall that shimmered like sparkling diamonds. He was breathless by the beauty of it all.

Justin found a quiet inlet by the sparkling stream to lay his head and took a rest. First, he observed his surroundings and noticed a nest settled high on a branch. A tiny cup-shaped bird's nest, the size of a walnut shell was resting in the shade of leaves surrounded by berries, grass, twigs and fluff. Justin heard the soft chirping of baby birds coming from the nest and from a distance he saw the mother bird feeding them. After a few moments, there was fluttering, then the mother and one baby bird departed the nest and flew to the north, the direction that their ancestors have always followed. Justin could still hear a faint chirping coming from the nest. He climbed up the tree with ease, he had learned well from Otorongo.

Gently, Justin approached the small nest. He peeked inside and was surprised to find the tiniest and most beautiful hummingbird he had ever seen. It appeared that the tiny hummingbird had been abandoned.

"I cannot fly!" cried the hummingbird. "My wings have not fully grown."

Justin realized that this might be one of Sasha's friends, but the power animals were supposed to help Justin through his journey. It seemed to him that he was the one that would have to help this little bird. Justin said, "hi little one, my name is Justin, I will help you."

"Hi, my name is Kinti," the tiny hummingbird said.

"You must be sad about your family leaving you behind!" Justin said with sadness in his voice.

"They didn't leave me behind," she said, "everyone is ready to journey on their own time. I need to allow myself to grow and gain my strength by drinking from the nectar of life."

"What is the nectar of life?" Justin questioned.

Kinti answered, "The nectar of life is the sweetness that life has to offer. Drinking from the sweetness of life gives us the courage to follow our dreams, and to embark on an epic journey, the journey of our growth."

Justin wondered how Kinti could find sweetness in abandonment. Justin did not understand the meaning of Kinti's message. He only saw a helpless baby bird, so he asked Kinti, "How can I help you?"

Excitedly Kinti told Justin, "It would be wonderful if while I wait for my wings to grow, you could carry me in the palm of one of your hands. I can show you which flowers have the best nectar to drink from and help me grow. Once I gain my strength I will be able to embark on my journey and meet my family again." Justin gladly accepted.

For the rest of the day Justin and Kinti explored the gardens. Kinti shared with Justin the beauty of Mother Earth. They enjoyed the flower meadows, and smelled the sweet aroma of lavender. They were delighted by the melodies of the many birds that filled the air. With Justin's help, Kinti was able to drink and feed from the most amazing exotic blooms.

Justin was inspired and grateful for every experience. The sweet nectar filled Kinti with joy and a sincere passion for life. Justin found himself feeling peaceful and happy by Kinti's energy. He gained appreciation for all the beauty of Mother Nature and the beauty that he was finding inside himself. Justin was drinking from the nectar of life and was transformed by it.

Justin and Kinti spent the night in the quiet garden. Lying on the cool grass, Kinti snuggled in the curve of Justin's neck. He felt Kinti's softness and warmth as they fell asleep peacefully together.

~

CHAPTER SEVEN

While Justin was deep in thought, he realized that Kinti had been the one helping him all along. Kinti had taught him to find the sweetness within himself, to find the courage to follow his own path. Kinti whispered, "You are never really alone in your journey, the spirits of your ancestors whisper to you in the wind. Listen to them and they will always guide you." At that moment a light breeze swirled around them and Justin listened to the messages in the wind.

Justin awoke the next morning, seeing Kinti in a wonderful mood. She was ready to embark on her flight to join her family. Justin was happy for her, although he was going to miss having his sweet friend around.

Kinti explained to Justin, "Mothers know when to release their children for the benefit of their growth. It is never easy to let go of the ones you love, but love goes beyond the boundaries of distance and separation. They are always with you in spirit, guiding you and sending you their best intentions for your happiness."

Justin asked Kinti, "Do you want me to join you until you find your mother?"

Kinti replied, "I am grateful for your company, but this is a journey I now need to experience alone. You have your own journey to embark upon; there is always sweetness available to you in every experience, when you look for it. You may have thought that I was a lonely, abandoned baby. The truth is that this experience gave me a great gift, it brought me the sweetness of your friendship."

"Ah, I will miss you Kinti...." Justin expressed sincerely.

Kinti took flight, and declared, "I will see you again!"

Although Justin felt sad seeing Kinti fly away, he also felt so much joy for his friend. This is what Kinti meant by releasing our loved ones and allowing them to follow their dreams.

While Justin continued on his journey, he made time to stop and smell the flowers... enjoying the sweetness of life.

CHAPTER EIGHT

Inspired by his new sense of life and determination, Justin listened to his inner knowing to lead the way. Justin began his walk towards *Luminous Mountain*. He longed to see his mother, no longer driven by desperation but by his love for her.

Justin looked forward to the journey he was about to take. He sensed this new path was the next step to a place of Enlightenment.

He travelled by the edge of a great ocean, arriving at a mountain after many hours. He remembered Sasha telling him about *Luminous Mountain*. Energetically he ran to the top of this mountain hoping to see his mother waiting for him. Great disappointment came over him at the realization that she was not there. He sat in silence, thinking what to do next. At that moment, Justin felt a great presence. High in the sky, coming from the east direction, where the sun was rising, he saw an Eagle approaching him.

The majestic bird was larger than Justin. The Eagle had a brown body with a white head and tail, and golden feet. Justin had never seen such a magnificent creature. The Eagle spoke, his voice was wise and commanded respect. "I have been waiting for you." With wonder and delight by his prominent presence, Justin was in awe. "Ah... I am Justin..." he said softly.

"Hello Justin, my name is Apuchin, I am the messenger of Great Spirit and I bring vision and clarity."

In a sad voice, Justin said, "I thought my mother would be here waiting for me."

Apuchin replied, "She waits for you at *Luminous Mountain*. I will take you there through the path of Enlightenment, the place of awakening to the universal truth and connection to spirit."

Justin mounted Apuchin's back, feeling the strong, muscular body of the Eagle and the softness of his feathers. Justin put his arms around the Eagle's neck and held on tight. Apuchin spread his splendid wings and took flight. Flying high into the sky, they soared with grace. Justin gazed out over the sensational landscape. He saw the blue oceans, lakes and rivers, the white snowy mountain peaks, the green and golden lands; all of Mother Earth's creations.

Apuchin spoke, "Justin, this is your last lesson in your journey, it holds great wisdom; practice seeing things from above; from a higher perspective. When you see through the eyes of the heart you will gain clarity and expand your vision to rise above any situation. You will be able to go beyond boundaries and limitations. When you are pushed out of the nest, spread your wings so you can fly with Great Spirit. Soar high up close to heaven and allow your heart and soul to be free."

Apuchin flew over the meadows and everything below looked tiny. Justin noticed a bright sparkle down below. He was thrilled to see the sparkle was Sasha's silky skin as she was basking in the sun. He remembered Sasha's lessons, that he had the power to release his wounds and renew himself. He called to her and she swirled in delight.

As they flew over the rainforest, Justin looked for Otorongo. He saw Otorongo running at a great speed and climbing up the edge of a cliff to see him. Otorongo and Justin's eyes met and there was an overwhelming connection between them. Otorongo had taught Justin to overcome fear and violence, and to walk the path of peace. Justin remembered overcoming his fear of the wolf by embracing her and her cubs.

Justin looked for his precious little friend, Kinti, as they flew over the magical garden, but did not see her. Justin recalled how he believed that Kinti was abandoned; instead Kinti had inspired his courage to become independent. Kinti proved to Justin that it did not matter how little you were, as long as you have determination, you could always follow your dreams. All of a sudden, he heard a friendly and tiny voice, "Hello." Justin turned his head in amazement, and saw Kinti zooming towards him. Justin cried joyfully, "Kinti! What are you doing here?" Flying up beside him, Kinti responded, "I was able to catch up with my family. See, they are over there! We are on our way to Canada." Justin replied, "Kinti, I will always carry your sweetness within me." Kinti gently fluttered in the curve of Justin's neck and then flew away.

Justin continued to soar with Apuchin in silence. He tried to see with the eyes of Eagle. He saw the smallest details, the bigger picture, and the real meaning of his journey. He practiced seeing from his heart; the place of compassion. His desire to improve and to go beyond the limitations of our physical world required no words. Justin embraced the flight and was grateful for the lesson he had been shown.

Justin's heart was filled with joy; his journey had been blessed with great friendships.

CHAPTER NINE

For a while, Justin held onto Apuchin, sensing his wisdom and power. Justin realized that all the lessons he had learned earned him the honor to fly with Eagle. Justin was no longer a passenger; he had become one with Apuchin. They soared in the great heavenly sky for a long time as one free-spirit.

At a distance, Justin could see a magnificent mountain. Glowing effects of soft pink and indigo hues wrapped around the high peaks of the mountain. The valley's soft glow contrasted with the brilliantly intense splashes of colorful trees and flowers. Rays of pure divine light came out from the heart of the mountain. He sensed feelings of peace, tranquility, and harmony that surrounded this sacred place.

Apuchin announced, "This is *Luminous Mountain*." Justin was captivated by this magical sight. He didn't want to blink his eyes in case the magic would fade away.

Apuchin swooped down gently and landed near the top of the mountain. Justin dismounted Apuchin and stepped on the moist ground.

With approval and admiration Apuchin expressed, "You have learned the flow of life, experienced the freedom and magic of spiritual flight. You have attained Enlightenment." Apuchin's words resonated with Justin. Apuchin's essence made Justin feel as though he was in the presence of Great Spirit. Justin put his arms around Apuchin's neck one last time and said, "Thank you." Apuchin returned the gesture by bowing his majestic head. Justin watched as Apuchin gracefully flew off disappearing into the heavens.

Justin gazed at Apuchin, admiring the beauty of his spirit.

Moments later, Justin became aware of a glowing light coming from the highest peak of the mountain. There was his mother, standing with a beautiful light around her; wearing a flowing gown, and her long beautiful hair blowing in the light breeze. She smiled and spread her arms to welcome him. "Mom!" Justin shouted happily. He ran to her and they embraced for what seemed an eternity. "I missed you so much, I am so happy we are together again!" Justin cried joyfully.

Justin shared with his mother all of his adventures with Sasha, Otorongo, Kinti and Apuchin. He told her of all the lessons he had learned from his power animal friends. Justin explained the journey he had to take to attain Enlightenment. Justin couldn't wait to go home and tell his sister all of his adventures and he was surprised how much he had missed her. Justin looked forward to seeing his dad and sharing with him his brave adventure. He believed that his father would be so proud of him.

His mother said, "My son, you have found the source of love, the *Divine Light* shines within you now."

Justin lay embraced in his mother's arms. Exhausted from his long journey, he fell asleep peacefully.

When Justin woke up, he realized he was no longer in the mountain but found himself back in the sunny meadows, lying on his back, in the tall green grass. He looked to his side and saw his mother beside him smiling back at him.

Justin was confused and exclaimed, "I must have been dreaming, I thought you had left!"

His Mother smiled and said, "I have been with you all along. I am always with you. You are never alone." Justin smiled peacefully.

A moment later, Justin looked high in the sky as an Eagle flew by...